# Out of Debtors' Prison

## A Roadmap for Debt-Free Living

### By Dr. Kurt Grosser

Abundant Freedom Press
Aurora, Colorado

## Out of Debtors' Prison

ISBN 13: 978-0-9776765-2-1
ISBN 10: 0-9776765-2-8

Cover design by Archer Ellison, Inc.

Interior design and editing by Cynthia Arbuckle

Printed in the United States of America
Please visit our Web site for other titles and contact information
www.AbundantFreedomMinistries.com

G&G Publishing, Inc.
Abundant Freedom Press
P.O. Box 461316 • Aurora, CO 80046

# Dedication

This book is dedicated to all who are striving to live in financial freedom. Freedom from the bondage of the financial limitations imposed by our economic system. Freedom to live the abundant life and in the prosperity promised in the Word of God.

2 Corinthians 3:17 (NASB)
Now the Lord is the Spirit; and where the Spirit of the Lord is, there is liberty.

# Acknowledgements

Special thanks to Kathy, my wife, and our children for their patience, understanding and endless encouragement.

# Contents

# Introduction

Spending beyond one's means has become a way of life. This is true for individual households, businesses, churches, and government units, small and large. As long as our spending habits reflect our attitude towards debt, we have nowhere to go but deeper and deeper into obligations. Often we forget that debt encumbers our future.

Debt has been around since ancient Biblical times. One was always admonished to pay back as quickly as possible if one had to borrow in the first place. Large purchases, such as land acquisitions, were financed. Every fifty years there was a year of jubilee in which all debts were settled or cancelled.

Credit cards were introduced in the 1920's. After World War II, the use of credit was accelerated to such an extent that today we seem to be beyond the point of no return.

## Household statistics

Sixty percent of American families actually spend more than their after-tax income.

Even more surprising is the fact that 32 million families spend more than $8,000 more per year than they earn.

If the average American family has over $8,000 in credit card debt at an interest rate of 18%, it will require more than 25 years and over $24,000 to pay it off. U.S. consumer debt, including credit card debt and auto loans, is at approximately $18,700 per household. (Source— Federal Reserve).

## Mortgage statistics

The average mortgage debt per household was approximately $49,000 in 1993. By 2004, the average mortgage debt per household had increased to over $100,000.

## The Church has failed the followers

Let's look at the reality of the average debt level in a congregation of 100 household units. Based on the above statistics, one can assume that the congregation as a whole has an average combined sum of individual debts in the range of $11,870,000. These numbers are staggering and scary. Debt encumbers our future. The devil has snuck in and deceived not only the individual members, but often also the pastors and the church as a whole, into believing debt is okay. But is it really?

What does the Word of God, or the Bible, say about debt? It says, "The borrower becomes the lender's slave." And it also says that "Christ came and set us FREE." It goes on to say, "Keep standing firm, and do not be subject to the yoke of slavery again."

Why is it that so many believe that borrowing is "normal" and fail to see that they have become slaves to the lender, or the system? Why have so many pastors not taught on what the Scriptures say about managing finances? Could it be that some pastors don't preach on finances because they don't want to appear to be "money hungry" (and thus fulfill the common stereotype)? Or could it be that some pastors fear offending or "running off" those who are currently giving?

Did you know that there are over 2,300 Scriptures dealing with finances? That is more than on any other subject. There are probably not more than 100 Scriptures dealing with tithing and giving. There is much said about debt, ownership versus stewardship, and God's desire to bless His people. It's not about money—it's about God. It is written that the sum of the Word of God is true and we should not be ashamed of the Gospel. In Matthew and Luke it says that we cannot serve God and mammon.

## Where and how does it end?

It's time for the church of God to take its stand, or take its place. Preach the whole Word to the congregation. Our God is merciful and forgiving. As soon as we turn around from this omission, and ask for forgiveness and direction based on God's Word, we are on the road to debt-free living. After all, when the day comes that we are asked to give an account of our stewardship, we must be ready. Let's not forget that God wants to bless His people abundantly!

## Is there a way out?

Yes, there is hope in the Lord. Just as He took us when we turned our lives over to Him, He will take us and lead us from this disastrous debt dilemma.

In this book, we provide a roadmap for debt-free living.

# Chapter 1: Debt—A Way of Life

**In This Chapter**

✳ Buy now, pay later

## Buy Now and Pay Later

How long do we keep buying everything we wish to have and charge it? Our economy is built on our spending habits. We are taught to buy now and pay later. We are enticed to buy things even while we stand in a check-out line. Usually, both sides of the check-out line are lined with things to buy. We must realize that sooner or later we have to pay for everything we buy on credit, plus interest. There is no free ride.

Often, we make decisions to buy, or not to buy, based on how much the monthly payment is and whether we think we can squeeze it in. We fail to examine alternatives to buying. For example, if we need a piece of equipment, many go out and buy what they need on credit. Then they use the equipment for one or two projects. The rest of the time they lie around, get older, depreciate, and become outdated. We probably would have been better off to rent the equipment in the first place.

Some rationalize that if they can squeeze in the payment, they are not overextended. They fail to consider what happens if they lose their job, or if there is some other major change. If you don't think that your level of debt is a problem, just get three payments behind and find out what happens. You will quickly realize that you are in debtor's prison. They will come after you to collect. They can repossess what you bought on credit, and sell it at a much lower and depreciated price. You will still be held responsible for the balance. These lessons are very painful.

I know of a young lady who leased a hail-damaged new car. She felt she could make the payments since she got a substantial discount due to the minor damage. Within six months, she lost her job and was unable to keep up with the payments. The leasing company repossessed the vehicle and sold it a huge discount. The proceeds were applied toward her lease commitment. She was taken to court and held accountable and a judgment was filed against her for the remaining balance.

Next time, before you are ready to buy and charge or finance whatever you think you want or need, consider alternatives. Could you rent the item first? For example, it is cheaper to rent a motor home to see whether you like it. Ask yourself how often you would have time to use it. Then consider the costs of ownership, such as license plates, insurance, parking fees, storage cost, repairs and maintenance, etc. compared to a rental cost when you would be able to use it.

Before you decide to take on more debt, you should calculate the all costs associated with the purchase. You don't want to buy something and then later find out that you must buy, or pay for, additional items which you initially failed to consider. A mistake like that could be haunting.

Instead of buying things on impulse and paying for them over a long time, learn to ask yourself why do you need this? Why do you "need" this item right now? What are some other alternatives? Ask yourself why you want to buy something now without having the money to pay for it currently. Why must I have this now? Why can it not wait until I have the money to pay for it? Soon you will conquer the "buy now and pay later" habit.

We have been taught to make minimum payments. Often times we still pay for items long after their use or benefit has expired. If you do make a decision to buy something on credit, you need to pay the debt off as soon as possible. That means make as large a payment as possible each month. By this you will save a considerable amount of interest and pay off the debt much sooner.

Another form of debt we often overlook is cosigning. When a friend or family member wants to buy on credit but is not able to qualify on their own, they ask someone to cosign. When you cosign, it is essentially letting someone else buy now and you will probably pay later. The shortest and best advice one can give regarding cosigning, is: Don't! Don't cosign! Why should you subject yourself to paying for someone else? They do not qualify by themselves in the first place. If they qualify by themselves and then lose their job, you could help them out. Consider alternatives. You might be able to help them buy and pay for a used vehicle rather than a brand new one. Usually, in every situation there are a number of alternatives to cosigning.

## Refinancing Your Home – Instant Bailout

Low interest rates have fueled a "refinancing" frenzy. Some run up their credit cards until they are maxed out. Then they refinance their homes to pay off the credit cards. Twelve to twenty four months later they are in the same spot. Their credit cards are once again maxed out only this time they are still paying for the previous balance through their higher mortgage. They repeat the same over and over again until the mortgage rates rise and eventually their debt load is greater than they can carry. The end result is either they must sell their home, or lose it in bankruptcy.

Refinancing a home is good when we can lower the payments and save interest. To refinance credit card debt should at most be a one time situation. It should not be an instant bailout. You would be better off to experience the consequences of credit card debt and the difficult payoff over time than to receive a "quick fix". There is no lesson learned in a quick fix. Without a firm understanding of why you "need" to buy on credit without having the funds, you most likely will repeat your past mistakes. You must have an understanding of what makes you buy on credit. You must conquer that problem. Only when you are firmly convinced that you will no longer "buy now and pay later", then refinancing makes sense. Without that conviction, you are setting yourself up to repeat the same. Remember, whatever you buy on credit must sooner or later be paid for with interest. There is no free ride. Either you go through the pain of paying your debts, or you go through the pain of losing everything and start all over again until these basic principles sink in.

## Unreasonable Credit Limits

Credit cards are a trap for most people. They all start out at some credit limit. Once you reach that limit, they usually increase it to the next level, then to the next, and so forth. If you continue to increase your debt limit, sooner or later you will reach a level where you cannot keep up. Then comes the next card and the next until you are in serious trouble.

It is not unusual for credit limits to exceed the annual income of the debtor. By that time it is way too late. You would be better off to stop and ask yourself why you buy something without having the money.

## High Interest

Banks and financial institutions send out credit cards like cookies. They want you to transfer your balances. They promise lower rates. But you should read the fine print. Often the lower rates apply only for a limited time. The final rates could end up being higher than the rates you paid in the first place. Remember the interest is not the issue. The issue is why do you buy now and pay later and in that process become a "prisoner" to the lender.

Interest always goes in cycles. For sometime it is low, or lower, and eventually it creeps higher. It always seems to catch with you at a time when it is least convenient. Some argue that certain interest is tax deductible, therefore it is good. Don't believe that argument. Here is an example that defeats this argument. Say you are in a 28% tax bracket. Assume your interest payments are deductible. You start out with $100.

Now you pay the $100 out in interest. You get a tax deduction and thereby receive the tax savings of $28. So you have $28. Now compare this to having $100 and paying no interest. You do not have a tax deduction and therefore pay $28 in taxes. You still have $72 left over. When comparing the two alternatives, you are better off paying no interest, even though it is tax deductible, because for every $100 you have $72 left over compared to $28.

## The Problem

Most households are overextended. They live from paycheck to paycheck. On payday the house payment or rent is paid, then comes the car payment or payments, groceries, utilities and other bills. By the time credit card payments are added, there is not enough to go meet ordinary needs before the next payday. To close the "gap" from one payday to the next, they use their credit cards. Many are two or three paychecks from bankruptcy.

When you ask any family if they could make it financially if they had no debt payment, you get the answer. If we had no debt payments, of course we would have enough. Then debt is the problem.

## Reality

Reality is that debt encumbers the future. Anything that is borrowed must be returned and paid pack some day. Even zero interest loans must be paid back. There is no free ride. Too many people bank on the future. They borrow blindly without considering the consequences.

## The Treadmill

Often times the truth is that our spending habits or cycle is like a treadmill. People get stuck without knowing how to make changes.

They accept the cycle as "normal" and without much hope. Credit cards are loaded to their maximum and other cards are added. Many have little or no hope of ever getting caught up. Then one day they refinance their home and wrap all credit cards into their mortgage. The only problem is that then the cycle begins again.

## Is There Another Way Out?

There is a way out. You do not need to stay on the treadmill. Bankruptcy is not the only answer. You can pay off your debts and still have enough to live on. How can this be true? The Bible tells us to examine our ways. We need to look inward to find out why we buy on credit. Why do we keep on doing the very thing we hate to do, such as buying on credit?

We must develop a desire to change our ways. God has a divine order to our finances. But, it takes a commitment to make changes. It takes team effort. A household divided against itself cannot stand, but a household united cannot fail. You can do it. Remember, with God all things are possible.

# Chapter 2: Debt—The Problem

### In This Chapter

* ❋ Definitions of debt

* ❋ Types of debt

* ❋ The underlying causes of debt

* ❋ Consequences of debt

For more than twenty years I have been asking people who attended our Bible studies on *Scriptural Principles for Financial Success* the following question: **As you reflect on your financial situation, if you had no debt payments to make would your income be sufficient for you to live on?** For more than twenty years the answer has been the same: **"If I had no debt, sure I would have enough... I would have plenty."** Then *debt* is the problem.

# Definitions from Easton's Bible Dictionary:

### Debt

The Mosaic law encouraged the practice of lending (Deut. 15:7; Ps. 37:26; Matt. 5:42); but it forbade the exaction of interest except from foreigners. Usury [collecting interest] was strongly condemned (Prov. 28:8; Ezek. 18:8, 13, 17; 22:12; Ps. 15:5). On the Sabbatical year all pecuniary [monetary] obligations were canceled (Deut. 15:1-11). These regulations prevented the accumulation of debt.

### Debtor

Various regulations as to the relation between debtor and creditor are laid down in the Scriptures.

(1.) The debtor was to deliver up as a pledge to the creditor what he could most easily dispense with (Deut. 24:10, 11).

(2.) A mill, or millstone, or outer garment, when given as a pledge, could not be kept over night (Ex. 22:26, 27).

(3.) A debt could not be exacted [demanded] during the Sabbatic year (Deut. 15:1-15).

For other laws bearing on this relation see Lev. 25:14, 32, 39; Matt. 18:25, 34.

**(4.) A surety [co-signor] was liable in the same way as the original debtor (Prov. 11:15; 17:18).**

### Loan

The Mosaic law required that when an Israelite needed to borrow, what he asked was to be freely lent to him, and no interest was to be charged, although interest might be taken of a foreigner (Ex. 22:25; Deut. 23:19, 20; Lev. 25:35-38). **At the end of seven years all debts were remitted [forgiven]. Of a foreigner the loan might, however, be exacted. At a later period of the Hebrew commonwealth, when commerce increased, the practice of exacting usury or interest on loans, and of surety-ship in the commercial sense, grew up. Yet the** exaction of it from a Hebrew was regarded as discreditable (Ps. 15:5; Prov. 6:1, 4; 11:15; 17:18; 20:16; 27:13; Jer. 15:10).

Limitations are prescribed by the law to the taking of a pledge from the borrower.

The outer garment in which a man slept at night, if taken in pledge, was to be returned before sunset (Ex. 22:26, 27; Deut. 24:12, 13). A widow's garment (Deut. 24:17) and a millstone (Deut. 24:6) could not be taken. A creditor could not enter the house to reclaim a pledge, but must remain outside till the borrower brought it (Deut. 24:10, 11). **The Hebrew debtor could not be retained in bondage longer than the seventh year, or at farthest the year of jubilee (Ex. 21:2; Lev. 25:39, 42),** but foreign sojourners were to be "bondsmen forever" (Lev. 25:44-54).

**Debt is an Obligation**—something by which a person is bound to do certain things, and which arise out of a sense of duty *(Webster)*.

**Debt:** 1.That which is due from one person to another, whether money, goods, or services; that which one person is bound to pay to another, or to perform for his benefit; thing owed; obligation; liability. 2. A duty neglected or violated; a fault; a sin; a trespass. *(dictionary.com)*

---

**Food for thought: the Hebrew word for "borrow" or "lend" in the Old Testament is also at times translated—"to join with" or "attached to". This seems to imply a spiritual bond that is established between a borrower-lender as the two parties are joined together in relationship.**

---

# Why do people use their credit cards so freely?

Some people rationalize that debt is okay as long as they can make the payments. This is faulty logic.

Don't they know that sooner or later debt will catch up with them?

The Bible reminds us of this inevitility throughout scripture. Habakkuk 2:6-7 is a good starting point.

### Habakkuk 2:6-7 (NASB)

*⁶"Will not all of these take up a taunt-song against him, even mockery and insinuations against him and say, 'Woe to him who increases what is not his—for how long—and makes himself rich with loans?' ⁷"Will not your creditors rise up suddenly, and those who collect from you awaken? Indeed, you will become plunder for them."*

Compare the following verses to the thoughts in Habakkuk 2:6-7:

### James 4:13-17 (NIV)

*¹³Now listen, you who say, "Today or tomorrow we will go to this or that city, spend a year there, carry on business and make money." ¹⁴Why, you do not even know what will happen tomorrow. What is your life? You are a mist that appears for a little while and then vanishes. ¹⁵Instead, you ought to say, "If it is the Lord's will, we will live and do this or that." ¹⁶As it is, you boast and brag. All such boasting is evil. ¹⁷Anyone, then, who knows the good he ought to do and doesn't do it, sins.*

### Proverbs 27:1 (NIV)

*¹ Do not boast about tomorrow, for you do not know what a day may bring forth.*

# Types of debt

- ❋ Consumer Debt
- ❋ Credit Cards
- ❋ Auto Loans
- ❋ Installment Loans
- ❋ Mortgages (personal residence, investment property)

---

### How long have credit cards been around?

According to the Encyclopedia Britannica, the use of credit cards originated in the U.S. during the 1920s, when individual companies, such as hotel chains and oil companies, began issuing them to customers for purchases made at their businesses. This use increased significantly after World War II.

---

# Borrowing has become a way of life

**We have been taught to buy now and pay later**—the catch is that we forget that we still have to pay it back, and not just pay it back—pay it back with interest.

**Example:**

Assume you buy something on credit for $1,000:

Assuming monthly payments of $50; it will take you two years or 24 months to pay it off and cost you $1200 interest included (most consumer debt carries 15% to 21% interest). You will have to earn approximately $1700 and then pay income tax, to have $1200 left over to pay off the debt.

This is a different way of looking at debt. Most times when people purchase on credit they ask themselves, "Can I afford the payment?" Instead, they should consider the effect of interest and the amount of money they will have to earn in order to pay off the debt.

**What have you learned from this new perspective?**

_____

_____

_____

_____

_____

_____

_____

## Remember: debt destroys and interest devours

The moment you borrow, you engage the "monster" called interest. It works against you 24 hours a day, seven days a week. It never stops until the debt is paid in full.

## Slogans of our time

* Buy now, pay later!

* Instant credit approval!

* Easy payments!

* Make no Payments until 20xx (next year) or even 20xx (the following year)!!

* Choose the any company "no hassle" card

* Zero % interest on balance transfers for life

* The card that pays you back

* It's everywhere you want to be

* Save 10% on your purchase today with an (any company) card!

* What's in your wallet?

* Priceless

Many people are enticed by these so-called deals. However, if you read the fine print, you will realize that you must follow some very specific rules to avoid penalties. If you do not, the penalty can be extreme.

These slogans are pervasive in the western culture. It is virtually impossible to go through a day without receiving emails, flyers, or phone calls, seeing billboards or commercials, or hearing jingles on your favorite radio station. Companies invest billions each year to entice us to buy their products, and these slogans are meant to be the bait that lures you in.

**How have you been affected by the slogans of our time?**

_____

_____

_____

_____

_____

_____

_____

_____

People take on debt thinking that their income will increase to cover payments. However, the average income after inflation is actually going down.

It is not the amount of money you have that is important; it is what you do with what you have. Often times when people find out that they will get a pay-increase, the money is "spent" or committed well before the increase shows up on the paycheck.

# Debt encumbers your future!

Overspending has become a problem as pervasive as over-eating!

| Year | Amount Overspent | Accumulated Interest | End of Year Balance |
|------|------------------|----------------------|---------------------|
| 1 | $1,200 | $110.21 | $1,310.21 |
| 2 | $1,200 | $382.01 | $2,892.22 |
| 3 | $1,200 | $710.20 | $4,802.42 |
| 4 | $1,200 | $1,106.48 | $7,108.90 |
| 5 | $1,200 | $1,584.96 | $9,893.86 |
| 6 | $1,200 | $2,162.71 | $13,256.57 |
| 7 | $1,200 | $2,860.31 | $17,316.88 |
| 8 | $1,200 | $3,702.62 | $22,219.50 |
| 9 | $1,200 | $4,719.67 | $28,139.17 |
| 10 | $1,200 | $5,947.72 | $35,286.89 |
| 11 | $1,200 | $7,430.53 | $43,917.42 |
| 12 | $1,200 | $9,220.92 | $54,338.34 |
| 13 | $1,200 | $11,382.76 | $66,921.10 |
| 14 | $1,200 | $13,993.06 | $82,114.16 |
| 15 | $1,200 | $17,144.88 | $110,459.04 |
| 16 | $1,200 | $20,950.54 | $122,609.58 |
| 17 | $1,200 | $25,545.69 | $149,355.27 |
| 18 | $1,200 | $31,094.11 | $181,649.38 |
| 19 | $1,200 | $37,793.59 | $220,642.97 |
| 20 | $1,200 | $45,882.82 | $267,725.79 |
| Total | $24,000 | $243,725.79 | $267,725.79 |

Consider the consequences of overspending $100 per month (or $3.29 per day). Assume a credit card rate of 19% compounded monthly for 20 years.

This illustration will show you how a little careless overspending can wreck you family's finances and rob you of your freedom.

Just think what overspending in larger amounts, or binge spending, will do to financial freedom.

**Do you overspend regularly? By how much?**
**Do you know why?**

_____

_____

_____

_____

_____

_____

_____

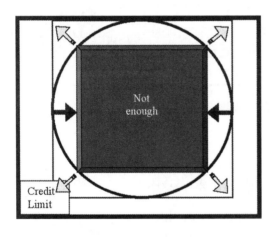

The circle represents our net income: For example, $3,000 income per month. But spending $3,500 per month until credit limit is reached (large square)

Assume cost of Household is $2,700 per month. Ultimate consequence - $800 payments and living on $2,200 per month. Shortfall of $500 is now covered by Credit Card, leading to ultimate disaster.

Do you see the cycle?

# Debt is a symptom of other underlying problems

The underlying root causes are usually one or more of the following:

- Greed

- Lack of contentment

- Lack of self-discipline

- Impatience

- Poor self-image

The problem with overspending is that you still have to pay the resulting debt at some time. Often the need for repayment comes when you can least afford it or when you least expect it.

**What are some of the underlying causes for buying on credit in your life?**

_____

_____

_____

_____

_____

_____

_____

## The underlying cause could also be a spiritual consequence

Consider the following verses:

### Malachi 3:8-11 (NLT)

[8] *"Should people cheat God? Yet you have cheated me! "But you ask, 'What do you mean? When did we ever cheat you?'" You have cheated me of the tithes and offerings due to me.* [9] *You are under a curse, for your whole nation has been cheating me.* [10] *Bring all the tithes into the storehouse so there will be enough food in my Temple. If you do," says the LORD Almighty, "I will open the windows of heaven for you. I will pour out a blessing so great you won't have enough room to take it in! Try it! Let me prove it to you!* [11] *Your crops will be abundant, for I will guard them from insects and disease. Your grapes will not shrivel before they are ripe," says the LORD Almighty.*

# Tithing = Blessing
# Not Tithing = Curse

### Deuteronomy 15:6 (NLT)

[6] *The LORD your God will bless you as he has promised. You will lend money to many nations but will never need to borrow! You will rule many nations, but they will not rule over you!*

### Deuteronomy 28:12 (NLT)

[12] *The LORD will send rain at the proper time from his rich treasury in the heavens to bless all the work you do. You will lend to many nations, but you will never need to borrow from them.*

His Blessing is that you will lend to many nations, but you will not need to borrow.

When we accept God's blessings, then there is no need to borrow because He promises to supply all our needs. When we don't believe in the blessings God promises in His Word, then we choose to operate under the curse by borrowing.

### Deuteronomy 28:44 Paraphrase

*Curses are that he (the unbeliever) will lend to you (that means you borrow), and he will become the head and you will become the tail.*

---

For a more thorough review of <u>blessings</u> read
Deuteronomy 28:1-14.

And for <u>curses</u> read Deuteronomy 28: 15-68.

---

### Proverbs 22:7 (NLT)

*⁷Just as the rich rule the poor, so the borrower is servant to the lender*

Once you discover the reason(s) why you take on debt, you can ask the Lord to deliver you from that affliction. Then, getting out of debt becomes easier.

**Ask the Lord to help you search your heart and show you why you are buying things on credit**

_____

_____

_____

_____

_____

_____

# Consider your ways!!

### *Haggai 1:5-11 (NLT)*

*[5] This is what the LORD Almighty says: Consider how things are going for you! [6] You have planted much but harvested little. You have food to eat, but not enough to fill you up. You have wine to drink, but not enough to satisfy your thirst. You have clothing to wear, but not enough to keep you warm. Your wages disappear as though you were putting them in pockets filled with holes!*

*[7] "This is what the LORD Almighty says: Consider how things are going for you! [8] Now go up into the hills, bring down timber, and rebuild my house. Then I will take pleasure in it and be honored, says the LORD. [9] You hoped for rich harvests, but they were poor. And when you brought your harvest home, I blew it away. Why? Because my house lies in ruins, says the LORD Almighty, while you are all busy building your own fine houses. [10] That is why the heavens have withheld the dew and the earth has withheld its crops. [11] I have called for a drought on your fields and hills—a drought to wither the grain and grapes and olives and all your other crops, a drought to starve both you and your cattle and to ruin everything you have worked so hard to get."*

### *Haggai 2:4-9 (NLT)*

*[4] But now take courage, Zerubbabel, says the LORD. Take courage, Jeshua son of Jehozadak, the high priest. Take courage, all you people still left in the land, says the LORD. Take courage and work, for I am with you, says the LORD Almighty. [5] My Spirit remains among you, just as I promised when you came out of Egypt. So do not be afraid.*

*[6] "For this is what the LORD Almighty says: In just a little while I will again shake the heavens and the earth. I will shake the oceans and the dry land, too. [7] I will shake all the nations, and the treasures of all the nations will come to this Temple. I will fill this place with glory, says the LORD Almighty. [8] The silver is mine, and the gold is mine, says the LORD Almighty. [9] The future glory of this Temple will be greater than its past glory, says the LORD Almighty. And in this place I will bring peace. I, the LORD Almighty, have spoken!"*

**Proverbs 14:8 (NLT)**

*[8] The wise look ahead to see what is coming, but fools deceive themselves.*

## Choose life and prosperity, not death and adversity!!

**Deuteronomy 30:15 (NLT)**

*[15] "Now listen! Today I am giving you a choice between prosperity and disaster, between life and death.*

**Deuteronomy 30:15 (NASB)**

*[15] "See, I have set before you today life and prosperity, and death and adversity;*

## What does God say about debt?

# Debt = Bondage
# No Debt = Freedom

## Consequences of borrowing

The borrower becomes the lender's slave.

**Proverbs 22:7 (NASB)**

*[7] The rich rules over the poor, And the borrower becomes the lender's slave.*

**Romans 8:13 (NASB)**

*[13] For if you live according to the flesh you will die; but if by the Spirit you put to death the deeds of the body, you will live.*

**Numbers 30:2 (NASB)**

*[2] "If a man makes a vow to the LORD, or takes an oath to bind himself with a binding obligation, he shall not violate his word; he shall do according to all that proceeds out of his mouth."*

### Job 24:9 (NLT) talks about infants being seized for debt

⁹*"The wicked snatch a widow's child from her breast; they take the baby as a pledge for a loan."*

It seems unthinkable in the American legal system that a baby would ever be seized for a debt. However, let's take a look at this verse a little more deeply. Perhaps it talks of losing something precious and valuable because of the bondage of debt. Perhaps you lose an important part of yourself.

**First, consider what is most precious to you
and has the greatest value in your eyes**

_____

_____

_____

_____

_____

_____

_____

Bondage to debt places you in the bonds of slavery. What this means is that someone else can make decisions for you if you default on your loan. It seems far-fetched, but imagine what would happen if you lost everything.

**Take some time to write your thoughts**

_____

_____

_____

_____

_____

_____

_____

_____

### 2 Kings 4:1 (NLT)

*¹ One day the widow of one of Elisha's fellow prophets came to Elisha and cried out to him, "My husband who served you is dead, and you know how he feared the LORD. But now a creditor has come, threatening to take my two sons as slaves."*

> Take some time to read the rest of the story recorded in 2 Kings 4. It is a great story of faith.

### Luke 16:13 (The Message)

*No worker can serve two bosses: He'll either hate the first and love the second, Or adore the first and despise the second. You can't serve both God and the Bank.*

### Deuteronomy 6:13-15 (NLT)

*¹³ You must fear the LORD your God and serve him. When you take an oath, you must use only his name. ¹⁴ "You must not worship any of the gods of neighboring nations, ¹⁵ for the LORD your God, who lives among you, is a jealous God. His anger will flare up against you and wipe you from the face of the earth."*

### Luke 14:28-30 (NLT)

[28]*"But don't begin until you count the cost. For who would begin construction of a building without first getting estimates and then checking to see if there is enough money to pay the bills?* [29]*Otherwise, you might complete only the foundation before running out of funds. And then how everyone would laugh at you!* [30]*They would say, 'there's the person who started that building and ran out of money before it was finished!'"*

### James 4:3 (NLT)

[3]*And even when you do ask, you don't get it because your whole motive is wrong—you want only what will give you pleasure.*

**Meditate on James 4:3 and write your thoughts**

_____

_____

_____

_____

_____

_____

_____

## The real world—and consequences for taking on debt

- We think we need things right now

- We are not patient enough to wait upon the Lord

- We buy on credit and then pray for the payments

**Your debt keeps you on a treadmill and robs you of your seed!!!**

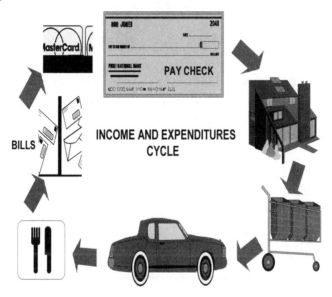

**Reflect on what we have learned so far—
what is your view of debt?
Do you consider debt to be bondage?**

_____

_____

_____

_____

_____

_____

_____

_____

Make a commitment to tithe and there will be no
need to borrow

### *2 Chronicles 31:10 (NASB)*

*[10]Azariah the chief priest of the house of Zadok said to him, "Since the
contributions began to be brought into the house of the LORD, we have*

*had enough to eat with plenty left over, for the LORD has blessed His people, and this great quantity is left over."*

Before purchasing, ask yourself: Is this something I really need or something I really want?

## On Cosigning—don't

**Proverbs 17:18 (NLT)**

[18]*It is poor judgment to co-sign a friend's note, to become responsible for a neighbor's debts.*

**Proverbs 22:26-27 (NLT)**

[26]*Do not co-sign another person's note or put up a guarantee for someone else's loan.* [27]*If you can't pay it, even your bed will be snatched from under you.*

**Have you ever cosigned for someone? What did you learn? What advice would you give to someone who is considering cosigning for someone else?**

_____

_____

_____

_____

_____

_____

_____

If you have already co-signed, pray about the situation, then remove yourself from the liability as soon as possible.

### Proverbs 6:1-5 (NLT)

*¹My child, if you co-sign a loan for a friend or guarantee the debt of someone you hardly know—²if you have trapped yourself by your agreement and are caught by what you said—³quick, get out of it if you possibly can! You have placed yourself at your friend's mercy. Now swallow your pride; go and beg to have your name erased. ⁴Don't put it off. Do it now! Don't rest until you do. ⁵Save yourself like a deer escaping from a hunter, like a bird fleeing from a net.*

### Proverbs 11:15 (NLT)

*¹⁵Guaranteeing a loan for a stranger is dangerous; it is better to refuse than to suffer later.*

## On Auto Loans

New car every four years: $18,000 with 10% down and 4% interest for 48 months.

Total cost of ownership: $42,957.

| Year | 1 | 2 | 3 | 4 |
|---|---|---|---|---|
| Gasoline | $1,200 | $1,200 | $1,200 | $1,200 |
| Oil Change | $120 | $120 | $120 | $120 |
| Maintenance | $0 | $0 | $0 | $150 |
| Repairs | $0 | $0 | $0 | $350 |
| License | $360 | $270 | $200 | $177 |
| Sales Tax 7.5% | $1,350 | $0 | $0 | $0 |
| Insurance | $950 | $950 | $950 | $950 |
| Loan Payment | $4,390 | $4,390 | $4,390 | $4,390 |
| Down Payment | $1,800 | $0 | $0 | $0 |
| Depreciation | $4,500 | $3,500 | $2,500 | $1,150 |
| Cost Per Year | $14,671 | $10,432 | $9,363 | $8,491 |

Same car, three years old: $7,500 cash purchase.

Total cost of ownership: $24,313.

| Year | 1 | 2 | 3 | 4 |
|---|---|---|---|---|
| Gasoline | $1,200 | $1,200 | $1,200 | $1,200 |
| Oil Change | $120 | $120 | $120 | $120 |
| Maintenance | $250 | $270 | $300 | $320 |
| Repairs | $350 | $500 | $600 | $700 |
| License | $150 | $130 | $110 | $90 |
| Sales Tax 7.5% | $563 | $0 | $0 | $0 |
| Insurance | $800 | $800 | $800 | $800 |
| Loan Payment | $0 | $0 | $0 | $0 |
| Down Payment | $7,500 | $0 | $0 | $0 |
| Depreciation | $1,000 | $1,000 | $1,000 | $1,000 |
| Cost Per Year | $11,933 | $4,020 | $4,130 | $4,230 |

Four Year Cost of Ownership

New Car      $42,957

Used Car     $24,313

Savings      $18,644

**What alternatives to buying on credit can you think of?**

_____

_____

_____

_____

_____

# On Installment Loans

Installment Loans are usually short-term loans of 3 to 5 years in duration. Consider your choices for a $20,000 loan at 9.5% interest. If you select a five-year loan, you will pay $420 per month and $5,200 interest over the life of the loan. Your total cash payments are $25,200. If you choose a three-year loan instead, your payments rise to about $640 per month. Total interest over the life of the loan is $3,060 making your total cash payment $23,060.

# On Mortgages

There are a variety of mortgage loan arrangements available today (i.e.: fixed, variable, 30-year, 15-year, etc.). The cost of mortgage payments and related tax savings for mortgage interest deductions is often close to actual rent payments. There are advantages and disadvantages to owning a home vs. renting a home.

Let's take a look…

## Some Advantages of Home Ownership

* Home ownership gives a sense of belonging and security

* Home ownership establishes a credit rating

* Home ownership can generate a sense of enjoyment and satisfaction

* If you have a fixed interest rate, your payments stay the same over the long-term

* Home ownership can create a valuable asset

* Tax savings for mortgage interest deductions

## Some Disadvantages of Home Ownership

* The homeowner must assume responsibility for financing, maintenance, care and improvements; renters on the other hand leave those responsibilities to the landlord

* Home ownership may require larger monthly expenditures compared to renting when you consider upkeep, improvements, taxes and insurance

* Real estate is subject to price fluctuations. The current cost may not be indicative of its future value.

The average length of time for home ownership before the property is sold or refinanced is 5 to 7 years. When you consider a $200,000 loan at 6% interest, in the first 5 years you pay principal and interest of $1,991.10 per month. The bank loans you the $200,000 and they collect all of it back plus $58,054.80 in interest. You assume all the risk of gain or loss on the sale of the property. Plus, you pay all insurance, taxes, and upkeep during the 5 years. However, history would show that in the past, values increased far more than the cost of ownership.

## On Refinancing—a slippery slope!

When you refinance your existing loan to get a better interest rate you should consider the refinancing charges. Generally, when the interest rate is reduced by 2%, it will save you money if you keep the home for at least three more years. However, if you refinance your mortgage to pay off existing credit card balances, you could be on a slippery slope.

It helps you temporarily to take the pressure off, but most of the time you are only digging a deeper hole.

Refinancing often turns out to be a quick fix. In six months to two years you are in trouble again. When you do this, you are actually spending your equity until there is nothing left.

Only when you have learned *why* you live beyond your means and have made a commitment to change your ways and get out of debt, only then is refinancing an option to reduce the interest rate.

# Chapter 3: Debt—How to Eliminate It

### In This Chapter

* ❋ Debt-free living

* ❋ Prayer for financial freedom

* ❋ Turning it over to God

* ❋ A financial plan

## Evaluating Your Financial Situation

When we begin to evaluate our **past** spending habit, every form of reasoning, defensiveness, and frustration will surface. When we examine our **present** financial position, depending on the result, we either feel defeated and discouraged, or proud and boastful of our accomplishments. God forgives us our past transgressions and we could not change anything of the past even if we wanted to. God's Word says that the old has gone and the new has come. That means that through Jesus Christ we have a new beginning.

We need God's guidance in evaluating our present financial situation. The Lord knows our hearts and motives and attitudes better than we do. It is for that reason that we must surrender ourselves to Him for guidance and direction.

We need to ask ourselves why we are willing to evaluate our financial situation. Is the reason to balance the numbers in our budget? Is the reason to solve a current financial crisis?

We know that **a budget, or spending plan, is only as good as the owner's willingness to follow it.** When we are sincere about wanting to change our old habits, and when we are willing to conform to live within the limits and flexibilities of our means, only then should we proceed.

I have seen numerous examples where people said they wanted a budget to start living within their means. They wanted God's guidance and direction. The problem is that they never really let go and let God. Once their present crisis passed they continued in their former ways. In Romans it tells us that the Word is the power of God and that revealed in it is His righteousness from faith to faith. That means that **it takes faith or belief in the Word from one end to the other.**

* ✳ Are we ready to accept and believe what God's Word says about our finances?

* ✳ Are we ready to act upon what the Word says?

* ✳ Are we willing to stand firm and not subject ourselves to our old ways?

> God knows our hearts and motives and attitudes better than we do. It is for that reason that we must surrender ourselves to Him for guidance and direction.

**Let us search our hearts**—The following Scriptures will give us some statements of policy to follow for this:

> When we begin to evaluate our past spending habits, every form of reasoning, defensiveness, and frustration will surface.

**Remember, the Lord is our source**—Jeremiah 17:5-10 states: "Thus says the Lord, cursed is the man who trusts in mankind and makes the flesh his strength, and whose heart turns away from the Lord. For he will be like a bush in the desert and will not see when prosperity comes, but will live in stony wastes in the wilderness, a land of salt without inhabitant. Blessed is the man who trusts in the Lord. For he will be like a tree planted by the water, that extends its roots by a stream and will not fear when the heat comes; but its leaves will be green, and it will not be anxious in a year of drought nor cease to yield fruit. The heart is more deceitful than all else and is desperately sick; who can understand it? I, the Lord, search the heart, I test the mind, even to give to each man according to his ways, according to the results of his deeds."

We need to build our patience and endurance—*a spending plan is only as good as the owner's willingness to follow it.*

## Setting our priorities

Before we begin to choose our financial priorities we need to remind ourselves of who we are in Christ and what that means. There are many Scriptures that reveal that God has a chosen plan (a path) for us. *Are we ready to accept and believe what God's Word says about our finances?*

What choices do we have when we are setting our priorities? God has made all our important choices for us, as we see in the above Scriptures. The only choice we have is to walk by our own free will in darkness and perish, or to choose His plan and path for us and succeed. When setting our priorities we must choose God and put Him first, then walk by His Word and He will do the rest.

There are some things we will have to do—such as living within the limits of our income. This can be done if we learn to rearrange our spending priorities.

It should also become a priority for us to get out of debt. We might review the list of things that we possess. We could sell those things which we do not need and apply the proceeds toward the debt.

## From debt management to surplus management— now!!

Prioritize your spending. Follow God's principles. The Bible tells us that the first portion belongs to God. The second portion belongs to the government, so pay your taxes. The third portion is to meet the needs of your own household. That requires that you carefully examine all expenditures and determine the need for each. The Bible warns us that he who does not meet the needs of his own household is worse that an unbeliever.

The fourth part, or what is left over after God, taxes, and your household needs, is surplus. That surplus should go to pay your creditors. So take responsibility and manage your finances and your surplus. Do not withhold repayment of your debts. Pay every dollar that is left over to the creditors.

The benefits of managing your finances are that there will be no need to borrow additional money. When your needs are met, and your spending plan includes contingencies and emergencies, then there will be no need to borrow. Once you stop borrowing and start reducing your debt, you are on the road to recovery.

For more information on developing a spending plan, see *Scriptural Principles for Financial Success and our Financial Success Workbook* in this series.

# Debt free living

It seems far fetched; even impossible. But with God all things are possible. You *can* be financially free, the chains of bondage *can* be broken, and you *can* take your rightful place as a child of God as the head and not the tail. In the last chapter we talked about how debt is the problem with our finances. God has the answers. Let's now take a look at the solutions from His Kingdom perspective.

As long as we accept debt as a way of life, we are deceived and remain in bondage.

Often we think that if we had just a little more money, we could make it. That is a lie.

Listen to this closely: *until you stop borrowing, you are not yet committed to getting out of debt.*

How to get debt under control and how to get out from under it?

Confess your transgressions

Make a commitment not to borrow again

Turn your debts over to God (but take responsibility)

Sell what you do not need

Do not withhold repayment

Beware of ever thinking, "Oh, that thing in my life doesn't matter much." The fact that it doesn't matter much to you may mean that it matters a great deal to God.

Do you protest that your heart is right with God, and yet there is something in your life He causes you to doubt? Whenever God causes a doubt about something, stop it immediately, no matter what it may be. Nothing in our lives is a mere insignificant detail to God

**Oswald Chambers My Utmost for His Highest**

# Confess your transgressions

As long as you are in debt you are in bondage. There is a spiritual bondage, which takes place between the one who lends and the one who borrows.

### Proverbs 22:7 (The Message)
*The poor are always ruled over by the rich, so don't borrow and put yourself under their power.*

**Isn't this true? When we borrow from the wealthy we are under their power, or become bound in the chains of bondage. When is the last time you felt that you were under the control of a lender?**

_____

_____

_____

_____

_____

### Proverbs 28:13 (NLT)
*[13]People who cover over their sins will not prosper. But if they confess and forsake them, they will receive mercy.*

We have to break the spiritual bondage between ourselves and our lenders. Since the spiritual realm precedes the physical manifestation, we need to ask God to let His UNCONDITIONAL forgiveness flow through our hearts to forgive and release the lender. Then we need to ask God to let His unconditional forgiveness flow through the heart of the lender and ask for the lender to forgive and release us. When the spiritual bondage is broken, the physical will manifest itself.

### Matthew 6:14-15 (The Message)

*"In prayer there is a connection between what God does and what you do. You can't get forgiveness from God, for instance, without also forgiving others. If you refuse to do your part, you cut yourself off from God's part."*

### Matthew 6:12 (NASB)

*<sup>12</sup>And forgive us our debts, as we also have forgiven our debtors.*

### Matthew 18:27 (NASB)

*<sup>27</sup>"And the lord of that slave felt compassion and released him and forgave him the debt."*

**Have you thought about forgiving your creditors? What would you say to them? Or, how would you go about doing that?**

_____

_____

_____

_____

_____

_____

_____

_____

### 2 Corinthians 2:10 (NLT)

*<sup>10</sup>When you forgive this man, I forgive him, too. And when I forgive him (for whatever is to be forgiven), I do so with Christ's authority for your benefit.*

### Ephesians 4:32 (NASB)

*<sup>32</sup>Be kind to one another, tender-hearted, forgiving each other, just as God in Christ also has forgiven you.*

### I John 1:9 (NASB)

*⁹If we confess our sins, He is faithful and just to forgive us our sins and to cleanse us from all unrighteousness.*

### Matthew 16:19 (NASB)

*¹⁹"I will give you the keys of the kingdom of heaven; and whatever you bind on earth shall have been bound in heaven, and whatever you loose on earth shall have been loosed in heaven."*

### Psalm 116:16 (NLT)

*¹⁶O LORD, I am your servant; yes, I am your servant, the son of your handmaid, and you have freed me from my bonds.*

### Romans 7:6 (NASB)

*⁶But now we have been released from the Law, having died to that by which we were bound, so that we serve in newness of the Spirit and not in oldness of the letter.*

# Prayer for financial freedom

Heavenly Father,

I come before You today in the Name of Your Son Jesus. I know that I am cleansed through His blood. So I stand before You perfect in Your Son, complete, lacking in nothing.

Father God, I confess that I have made many mistakes financially and as a result, I am in bondage with many people and creditors. So today, I turn over the entire mess, just as You instructed us to do. I commit unto You all of my belongings, my assets, my liabilities, my income and my expenses. They are Yours. I trust You completely. I know You will take care of **all** of my needs from this point forward. Please guide me and direct me in everything I do, everything I speak and in every step I take. From this day forward I am working for You, under Your guidance and direction. My aim is to do everything unto You, to please You and to assist others in everything I undertake.

Lord God, I now bring Your words with me, as I pray to be freed from the bondage of finance so I can serve You. Your word says that whatever

I bind on earth shall be bound in heaven and whatever I loose on earth shall be loosed in heaven. Spirit of GREED, spirit of WANT, spirit of IDOLATRY and spirit of COVETOUSNESS, I come against you in the Name of Jesus. I rebuke you in the Name of Jesus. I bind you with the blood of Jesus and command you IN HIS NAME to return to the darkness where you came from. I also come against the spirit of DEBT in the NAME OF JESUS. I rebuke you in the Name of Jesus and bind you with His blood. IN HIS NAME, I release you from your assignment against me and render you totally powerless. It is written that you spirits of darkness have been defeated by Jesus a long time ago and no longer have any say in my life. Now, to fill the vacant places in my heart, I release the spirits of LOVE, WISDOM, GRATEFULNESS, CONTENTMENT, TITHING and GIVING. I bind those godly spirits to my heart to guide me and direct me in every decision I make and every step I take. I thank You Father in Jesus Name.

Father God, I now would like Your help in setting me free from the financial bondage of all my creditors. I have listed each and every name of my creditors. In Jesus Name I ask that You now flow Your unconditional *forgiveness* from Your throne in heaven and cleanse my heart as I fully *forgive* and *release*.

I also ask that You flow Your unconditional *forgiveness* and *release* from Your throne in heaven and cleanse (John's) heart, as he completely forgives and releases me. We are both free and no longer encumbered spiritually. (Repeat for each and every creditor).

Thank You Father God, in Jesus' Name, for setting me completely free.

*Now make a commitment to pay back every obligation as quickly as possible.*

## Make a commitment not to borrow again

When you make a true commitment to get out of debt without borrowing again— this is true repentance, and you will begin to feel a freedom and peace that is difficult to describe.

*A TRUE commitment leaves no other option!*

Satan does not want to see God glorified in your life, nor for you to have freedom and peace, so he will put pressure on you to stay in debt or to get back in debt. The best way to keep the pressure off is to systematically pay off all old obligations and trust God to supply all your needs.

Although you have made a commitment to get out of debt, it will only be meaningful if you agree not to borrow again. If you are looking for God to bail you out and immediately borrow again, it will not work. God knows the intentions of our hearts.

### Galatians 6:7 (NASB)

*7Do not be deceived, God is not mocked; for whatever a man sows, this he will also reap.*

Borrowing can be avoided if you plan ahead

### Luke 14:28-30 (NASB)

*28"For which one of you, when he wants to build a tower, does not first sit down and calculate the cost to see if he has enough to complete it? 29Otherwise, when he has laid a foundation and is not able to finish, all who observe it begin to ridicule him, 30saying, 'This man began to build and was not able to finish.'"*

**We have all done it. Can you remember a time when you had to spend more than you intended to, simply because you did not plan ahead?**
**What was the outcome?**

_____

_____

_____

_____

_____

_____

_____

_____

_____

## Questions to reflect upon

Now having studied some of the Scriptures which warn you about being in debt, why do you think that God included such warnings for His people? Perhaps indebtedness inhibits our ability to take part in His plans for us.

**What do you think?**

_____

_____

_____

_____

_____

_____

_____

**Why are you committed to getting out of debt (remember—a true commitment leaves no other option)?**

_____

_____

_____

_____

_____

_____

### Can you agree not to borrow again, no matter what?

_____

_____

_____

_____

_____

_____

_____

### Why is cosigning, in principal, the same as borrowing?

_____

_____

_____

_____

_____

_____

_____

**Over the next seven days, return to the previous Scriptures and meditate on each one for three to five minutes. Write down any personal insights in the space below or in your journal**

_____

_____

_____

_____

_____

_____

_____

# Turn your debts over to God (but take responsibility)

## Turn it over

It is of utmost importance to remember that we are to turn everything over to God. However, we must take responsibility for our actions. Our freedom is a past event, but it is also a process. Renewal is often God's way of refocusing our eyes on Him in all areas of our lives.

# GOD

**We Cannot At the
Same Time Focus on
GOD & Our Problem**

| **WE** | → | **PROBLEM
(DEBT)** |
| --- | --- | --- |
| | ← | |

**IF WE FOCUS ON OUR FINANCIAL PROBLEMS,
THEY WILL IN TURN CONSUME US**

While we focus on a problem, we tend to worry so much about
it that we forget to focus on God.
What problems have consumed you in the past?

_____

_____

_____

_____

_____

_____

_____

_____

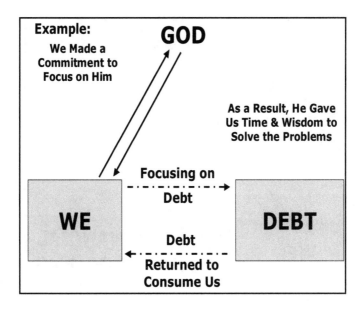

When we learn to focus on God and release our debt to Him through prayer, He gives us wisdom and understanding to solve the problem of debt.

**Describe what it looks like when you can only see debt in the rearview mirror of your life, while looking upon the glory of God?**

_____

_____

_____

_____

_____

_____

_____

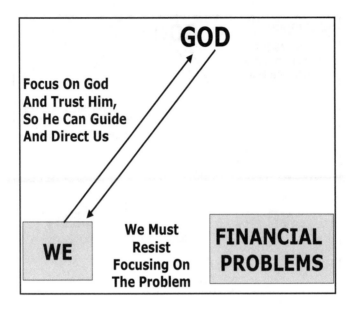

Focus on God. Look for Scriptures that talk about similar problems and solutions (that is what we are doing now). God will guide and direct us in solving the problems.

**In the Old Testament, the people were reminded to remember how God had helped them through difficulty. How has God helped you in the past?**

_____

_____

_____

_____

_____

_____

_____

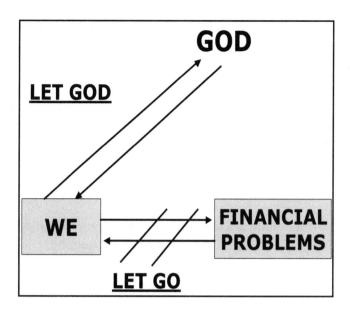

Let go of your problems and let God help you. Seek His Word for answers. God and His Word are the same—they cannot be separated.

**How does it feel to let go of a problem and let God handle it?**

_____

_____

_____

_____

_____

_____

_____

_____

Let go and let God—it has become a favorite saying of Christians everywhere. Actually doing it, however, takes practice and persistence. Paul instructed the Church in Corinth to take every thought captive so that it is obedient to Christ (2 Cor. 10:5), and that is what we must do with our fearful thoughts about our debts. It literally means that we should stop ourselves as soon as the fearful thought enters our mind and say "I have given this to Christ, and I refuse to worry about it. I trust that He will show me how to get through this."

**What problems have you experienced in the past as you tried to let go of your problems or fears?**

_____

_____

_____

_____

_____

_____

_____

# Trust is Unwavering Faith

Trust in the Lord with all your heart

### *Proverbs 3:5-6 (NASB)*

*⁵Trust in the LORD with all your heart And do not lean on your own understanding. ⁶In all your ways acknowledge Him, And He will make your paths straight.*

### Hebrews 6:12 (NLT)

<sup>12</sup> *Then you will not become spiritually dull and indifferent. Instead, you will follow the example of those who are going to inherit God's promises because of their faith and patience.*

In any relationship, trust takes time to build. The Bible commands us to trust God, and this begs the question: How can we trust someone that we do not know? God wants us to know Him and the Bible is His way of revealing Himself to us. If we want to know Him, we must read His Word.

**If we really want to get to know God, what questions can we ask Him about Himself— need help? What would you ask a person you were getting to know?**

_____

_____

_____

_____

_____

_____

_____

# Lean on Him

Call upon Him for help and strength

### Psalm 50:15 (NASB)

[15]*Call upon Me in the day of trouble; I will deliver you, and you shall glorify Me."*

### Psalm 37:5 (NASB)

[5]*Commit your way to the Lord, Trust also in Him, And He shall bring it to pass.*

### Ecclesiastes 7:14 (The Message)

*On a good day, enjoy yourself; On a bad day, examine your conscience. God arranges for both kinds of days So that we won't take anything for granted.*

**Meditate on Ecclesiastes 7:14 and write
down your thoughts.**

_____

_____

_____

_____

_____

_____

_____

# Take responsibility

A plan to become debt free would include a program to pay off existing debt.

### Numbers 30:2 (NASB)

*²"If a man makes a vow to the LORD, or takes an oath to bind himself with a binding obligation, he shall not violate his word; he shall do according to all that proceeds out of his mouth."*

# Keep your word; God will help you

### Matthew 18:19-20 (NASB)

*¹⁹"I also tell you this: If two of you agree down here on earth concerning anything you ask, my Father in heaven will do it for you. ²⁰For where two or three gather together because they are mine, I am there among them."*

### 2 Corinthians 9:8 (NASB)

*⁸And God will generously provide all you need. Then you will always have everything you need and plenty left over to share with others.*

**Why do you think it's important to take full responsibility for your debts?**

_____

_____

_____

_____

_____

_____

# Sell what you don't need

Sell those things which you do not need and apply the proceeds toward your debts. Take a look around you. The debt you have accumulated was because you bought something. Take a look in your closets, garage, and basement then make a list of those things that you have not used in six months or a year. If you have not used some items, ask yourself why you are keeping them? Do you really need them? If not, why don't you sell them and apply the proceeds toward your debts.

In the future, when you need an item consider renting it rather than buying it.

Liquidate investments and apply the proceeds toward your debts.

Remember:

## Your best investment ... is your DEBT!

For example:

A bank is paying you 4% interest on your savings account. The same bank is charging you 18% interest on your credit card. If you take from your savings account to pay off the credit card debt, you are earning 18% on your money, because if you leave it in the savings account you will only make 4% on it.

First consider what the pressure of your debt feels like. Write down the feelings that you have.

_____

_____

_____

_____

_____

_____

_____

Then imagine what the freedom will feel like
when you have paid off your debt.
Write down your thoughts here.

_____

_____

_____

_____

_____

_____

_____

_____

# Do Not Withhold Repayment

We have been taught to pay minimum payments only. That is wrong. If you have more, pay more. Pay as much as you can.

### Proverbs 3:27-28 (TLB)

*27-28Don't withhold repayment of your debts. Don't say "some other time," if you can pay now.*

### 2 Kings 4:1-7 (NASB)

*1Now a certain woman of the wives of the sons of the prophets cried out to Elisha, "Your servant my husband is dead, and you know that your servant feared the LORD; and the creditor has come to take my two children to be his slaves." 2Elisha said to her, "What shall I do for you? Tell me, what do you have in the house?" And she said, "Your maidservant has nothing in the house except a jar of oil." 3Then he said, "Go, borrow vessels at large for yourself from all your neighbors, even empty vessels; do not get a few. 4"And you shall go in and shut the door behind you and your sons, and pour out into all these vessels, and you shall set aside what is full." 5So she went from him and shut the door behind her and her sons; they were bringing the vessels to her and she poured. 6When the vessels were full, she said to her son, "Bring me another vessel." And he said to her, "There is not one vessel more." And the oil stopped. 7Then she came and told the man of God. And he said, "Go, sell the oil and pay your debt, and you and your sons can live on the rest."*

The widow sought godly advice when she had a crisis with her debts. But also notice that in verse 7, when she had an abundance, she sought godly advice again to find out what to do with it.

### Proverbs 21:20 (NASB)

*20There is precious treasure and oil in the dwelling of the wise, But a foolish man swallows it up.*

Based on the story above and Proverbs 21:20, it seems that sometimes the "precious treasure" or "oil" that will help us to pay off a debt is right under our nose. For some of us, the possessions that we already have might be worth enough to pay off all of our debts. For others of us, the skills or talents that we are blessed with could be a source of income. But notice, the woman had to be willing to give up the oil when Elijah asked her what she had in the house. She did not say, "Your maidservant has nothing in the house…except for some oil which you can't have because I am making my favorite meal today for my family and it requires all the oil that I have."

**What "oil" do you have in your house? Are you willing to give it up or will you "swallow it up?"**

_____

_____

_____

_____

_____

_____

_____

### Matthew 18:23-27 (TLB)

*23 "For this reason, the Kingdom of Heaven can be compared to a king who decided to bring his accounts up to date with servants who had borrowed money from him. 24 In the process, one of his debtors was brought in who owed him millions of dollars. 25 He couldn't pay, so the king ordered that he, his wife, his children, and everything he had be sold to pay the debt. 26 But the man fell down before the king and begged him, 'Oh, sir, be patient with me, and I will pay it all.' 27 Then the king was filled with pity for him, and he released him and forgave his debt.*

**Notice**

- ❋ The servant *confirmed* the debt
- ❋ He promised to pay it back
- ❋ The king forgave the debt

**How do these verses apply to your own situation?**

_____

_____

_____

_____

_____

_____

_____

# A plan for getting out of debt

Ask yourself how long it will take to get caught up and get out of debt, and most people quit before they even started. The answer is usually five to seven years, but often even much longer. Don't give up!!! First of all, unless we change our ways, there is no possible way of getting out of debt. *The system is designed to keep you in it.*

But – whom do you believe? – God's Word says that Christ came to set you free. (Galatians 5:1) The freedom that Christ gives us includes freedom from all debt.

You need a plan! The good news is if you earnestly seek the Lord's help, and work hard to pay off your debt you will pay it off faster than you think!

# Step 1

Make a commitment to get out of debt. Remember—true *commitment* leaves no other option!

# Step 2

Make a commitment not to borrow again, no matter what.

# Step 3

Prioritize your spending

First, pay your tithe

Second, pay your taxes

Third, meet the needs of your household (that requires a budget)

Fourth, apply the rest toward your debt (you should be out of debt within six months to two years).

But remember – Stop Borrowing—it is not an option.

If you don't take care of the first three parts before paying toward your debt, you will always be vulnerable to be short of some real need and you will continue to buy on credit. The key is to determine your *needs*, and provide for them. Then there will be no reason to have to borrow or charge in the future. It is when you stop borrowing all together that you will be on the road to freedom.

Our *Financial Success Workbook* in this series provides step-by-step instructions on how to determine your needs!

# Make extra payments as often as you can!

A plan to become debt free would include a program to pay off existing debt. Remember it took us years to get into the situation we are in, so it will take some time to get our situation back in order. When making extra payments on debt, it is wise to reduce debt which bears the highest interest rate first. When an account is paid off, then shift that payment and the extra payment to another account until they are all paid off.

## Examples of extra payments

### Early Pay-off of a Home Mortgage

Facts: $175,000 mortgage at 7% over 30 years (360 months) = $1,165.23/month.

| Regular Payment | Extra Payment | Total Payment | Months to Pay-off | $ Savings | Payments Saved |
|---|---|---|---|---|---|
| $1,165.23 | --- | $1,165.23 | 360 | --- | --- |
| $1,165.23 | $10.00 | $1,175.23 | 350 | $11,652.30 | 10 Months |
| $1,165.23 | $25.00 | $1,190.23 | 336 | $27,965.52 | 2 Years |
| $1,165.23 | $50.00 | $1,215.23 | 315 | $52,435.35 | 3 Yrs 9 Mos |
| $1,165.23 | $100.00 | $1,265.23 | 283 | $89,722.71 | 6 Yrs 5 Mos |

Facts: $175,000 mortgage at 7% over 15 years (180 months) = $1,572.95/month.

| Regular Payment | Extra Payment | Total Payment | Months to Pay-off | $ Savings | Payments Saved |
|---|---|---|---|---|---|
| $1,572.95 | — | $1,572.95 | 180 | — | — |
| $1,572.95 | $10.00 | $1,582.95 | 178 | $3,145.90 | 2 Months |
| $1,572.95 | $25.00 | $1,597.95 | 175 | $7,864.60 | 5 Months |
| $1,572.95 | $50.00 | $1,622.95 | 170 | $15,729.50 | 10 Months |
| $1,572.95 | $100.00 | $1,672.95 | 161 | $29,886.05 | 1 Yr 7 Mos |
| | | | | | |

# Alternatives to purchase a car on credit

**Historical Way of Buying a Car**

* Buy car for $15,000

* Trade-in Old car

* 48 payments of $400/month

RESULT – In 4 years you are driving an "old" car and need to buy a new one.

**Recommended Way of Buying a Car**

⁕ Save $400 for 6 months

⁕ Trade Old Car in (Trade Up) with $2,400 Cash

⁕ Save $400/month for 6 months (Or More)

⁕ Trade up With Cash

Result—in less than four years you will be driving a "new car"—paid in full!

# Chapter 4: Implementing Your Plan

**In This Chapter**

* Test your attitude about debt

* Assess your income and spending habits

* Apply a step-by-step approach to eliminating all of your debt

Debt free living is closer than you think. You can do it. Implement your plan.

Start now and win the battles, then you will win the war.

Take this road to freedom from debt. Once free, do not permit yourself to be lured into debt again. Consider alternatives and stay ahead of the game.

## Test your attitude about debt

* Debt destroys

* Interest devours

* God wants to break the curse of debt (which leads to poverty).

### What is your attitude about debt?

_____

_____

_____

_____

_____

_____

_____

Make a decision to change. Work hard to get out of debt.

### What changes have you noticed in your attitude about debt?

_____

_____

_____

_____

_____

**At this point, what steps do you think you need to take to get out of debt?**

_____

_____

_____

_____

_____

_____

_____

Make a commitment to get out of debt.

Eliminate all excuses—acknowledge the problem, don't deny it.

**What excuses have you used in the past?**

_____

_____

_____

_____

_____

_____

_____

### How can you eliminate those excuses from your life?

_____

_____

_____

_____

_____

_____

_____

_____

Overcome obstacles. Fear has no place in your life. Don't allow fear to rob your faith.

Most fears are the result of life experiences. When you allow fears to control your life, you become a prisoner of those fears.

### What obstacles can you identify in your life?

_____

_____

_____

_____

_____

_____

### What can you do to eliminate them?

_____

_____

_____

_____

_____

_____

Replace bad habits with good habits.

### What are some of your debt-related spending habits?

_____

_____

_____

_____

_____

_____

_____

## What can you do to change them?

_____

_____

_____

_____

_____

_____

_____

_____

## What are some good habits that you can substitute?

_____

_____

_____

_____

_____

_____

_____

# Assess your income and spending habits

## How can you increase your income?

Ask God to give you wisdom to use your talents to earn extra income to apply toward existing debts.

Here are a few possibilities:

Evaluate your options -

- ❋ work overtime
- ❋ ask for a pay raise
- ❋ work extra to get that bonus
- ❋ get a part-time job
- ❋ other family members work
- ❋ garage sale
- ❋ tutoring
- ❋ paint houses
- ❋ repairing houses
- ❋ start a small business
- ❋ consulting
- ❋ house cleaning
- ❋ lawn service

Place a check mark next to any of these possibilities.

**What can you do to begin?**

_____

_____

_____

_____

_____

_____

_____

_____

# Apply a step-by-step approach to eliminating your debts

Reduce your standard of living to allow the maximum to be applied toward reducing your debt. Sacrifice a little and get out of debt a lot faster.

Ask God to give you creative ways to sell what you do not need and apply the proceeds toward your debt.

## What are some alternatives to your current costs?

Here are some options:

* ❋ Do you price-shop?

* ❋ Could you reduce or eliminate some telephone charges?

* ❋ Could you eat out less frequently?

* ❋ What could you give up on a temporary basis?

* Could you move and pay less rent?

* Could you adjust your insurance costs?

**Which of these alternatives will work for you?**

_____

_____

_____

_____

_____

_____

_____

_____

## Evaluate your options

Money does not drop out of heaven; God gives us the ability to be prosperous at anything we put our hands to (work). God wants us to be able to meet the needs of our household. God wants good stewards.

* Before you buy anything, ask yourself if you really *need* it now?

* Consider alternatives.

* Choose alternatives and save.

* Cut costs where you can.

* Reduce your standard of living temporarily to allow for a monthly debt reduction program.

＊ Simplify your life—a debt free life is a simplified life.

＊ Contentment is the key. Pray that the Lord bless you with a spirit of contentment.

As discussed in Chapter 3, prioritize your spending:

1.  God's portion—the tithe

2.  Government's portion—taxes

3.  Your household needs

4.  Apply the *surplus* toward your debt

## Become a surplus manager instead of a debt manager

These spending priorities are God's divine order to manage your finances. They are discussed in greater detail in our Bible study guide *Scriptural Principles for Financial Success.*

You can determine your household needs and achieve remarkable flexibility in your spending, when you follow the *Financial Success Workbook,* a spending plan that *applies* God's principles to your finances.

## Set attainable goals

Goals need to be specific, solid and serious. Goals should have a deadline. For example: "I am committed to getting out of debt within two years."

Goals require:

＊ Prayer

＊ Courage

＊ Obedience

＊ Determination

* Positive attitude

* Patience

* Persistence

## Do you have a "team" buy-in?

For a plan to work, it takes the help and cooperation of all household members. It would be difficult for one member to try to get out of debt while the other still adds to debt.

Remember—a house divided against itself will not stand, but a house united cannot fail.

## Refinancing?

Only if your temptation to use credit cards is gone for good!

## Getting off the Financial Treadmill

Live within your means.

Work for it, and then buy it.

## Taking control over your finances

If you don't, someone else will take control over you.

Become the Steward God called you to be.

* Take Responsibility

* Be Accountable

* Be Persistent

# Apply a step-by-step approach to eliminating all of your debts

### Step 1—List all of your debts

Using the Debt Analysis Schedule that follows, list all of your debts precisely, specifically, and completely. Leave column 5 blank until you get to Step 2.

## Debt analysis schedule

Write down each debt. In column 1 write the total balance due; in column 2 write the interest rate the lender is charging you; in column 3 write the monthly payment amount you are currently paying; in column 4 divide the balance due by the payment per month (column 1 divided by column 3); prioritize your debt payoff (to be discussed in more detail later).

# Debt analysis schedule

| | Balance Due | Interest Rate | Payment Per Month | Time Until Payoff | Payoff Priority |
|---|---|---|---|---|---|
| **Installment Debts Credit Cards (creditor)** | | | | | |
| | | | | | |
| | | | | | |
| | | | | | |
| | | | | | |
| | | | | | |
| **Bank Loans (creditor)** | | | | | |
| | | | | | |
| | | | | | |
| | | | | | |
| | | | | | |
| | | | | | |
| | | | | | |
| **Other Loans, Notes, & Mortgages (creditor)** | | | | | |
| | | | | | |
| | | | | | |
| | | | | | |
| | | | | | |
| | | | | | |
| **Other Loans & Notes (creditor)** | | | | | |
| | | | | | |
| | | | | | |
| | | | | | |
| | | | | | |
| **Unpaid Bills (creditor)** | | | | | |
| | | | | | |
| | | | | | |
| | | | | | |
| | | | | | |

Total   T _____

Total Liabilities   T _____

## Step 2—prioritize your debt payments

When you prioritize your debt payments, eliminate consumer debt first, then mortgages. For example, if you have several credit cards, auto loans, and mortgages, you should target your credit card balances first. Once the credit cards balances are eliminated, target the auto loans. Finally, target the mortgages for payoff.

Now go back to the Debt Analysis Schedule and fill in column 5– "pay-off priority". Using the information listed on the Debt Analysis Schedule prioritize creditor balances which you want to target for elimination based on the interest rate or account balance. The highest interest rates should have the greatest pay-off priority*.

*Another way of prioritizing your debt repayment is to pay-off the account which has the lowest balance first. By applying all extra payments toward that account it can be eliminated quickly. Then there will be more left over to apply to the next lowest balance account to eliminate it as well.

Choose your preferred method of prioritizing and go for it!

## Step 3—keep a Record of Your Progress

Use the Goal Schedule that follows to set pay-off goals at the *beginning of each month*. We have included three copies of the Goal Schedule to get you started.

At the *end of each month*, track your progress. Use the Progress Management Debt Reduction Schedule to track your *actual* success each month. It will also help you see clearly how quickly your debt is decreasing.

# GOAL SCHEDULE
## MONTH_____

Income (from all sources)               $_____

Expenditures:
   **Tithes**               $_____
   **Taxes**               $_____
   **Household Needs** $_____

   **Total Expenditures**               $_____

Surplus (subtract expenditures from income)     $_____

## Surplus Applied to Debt Repayment:
## Creditor:

_____     $_____
_____     $_____
_____     $_____
_____     $_____
_____     $_____
_____     $_____
_____     $_____
_____     $_____
_____     $_____
_____     $_____

**Total Debt Reduction**               $_____

# GOAL SCHEDULE
## MONTH_____

Income (from all sources)            $_____

**Expenditures:**
   Tithes                    $_____
   Taxes                     $_____
   Household Needs $_____

   Total Expenditures        $_____

**Surplus** (subtract expenditures from income)    $_____

## Surplus Applied to Debt Repayment:
## Creditor:

_____    $_____
_____    $_____
_____    $_____
_____    $_____
_____    $_____
_____    $_____
_____    $_____
_____    $_____
_____    $_____
_____    $_____

**Total Debt Reduction**        $_____

# GOAL SCHEDULE
## MONTH_____

**Income** (from all sources)          $_____

**Expenditures:**
   **Tithes**            $_____
   **Taxes**            $_____
   **Household Needs** $_____

   **Total Expenditures**          $_____

**Surplus** (subtract expenditures from income)          $_____

**Surplus Applied to Debt Repayment:**
**Creditor:**

_____          $_____
_____          $_____
_____          $_____
_____          $_____
_____          $_____
_____          $_____
_____          $_____
_____          $_____
_____          $_____
_____          $_____

**Total Debt Reduction**          $_____

## Progress Management Debt Reduction Schedule

| Month | Total Income | Expenditures Tithes | Taxes | HH Needs | Surplus | Debt Reduction | Remaining Debt | Check If No New Debt |
|---|---|---|---|---|---|---|---|---|
|  |  |  |  |  |  |  |  |  |
|  |  |  |  |  |  |  |  |  |
|  |  |  |  |  |  |  |  |  |
|  |  |  |  |  |  |  |  |  |
|  |  |  |  |  |  |  |  |  |
|  |  |  |  |  |  |  |  |  |
|  |  |  |  |  |  |  |  |  |
|  |  |  |  |  |  |  |  |  |
|  |  |  |  |  |  |  |  |  |

# *Freedom from debt at last!*

# Other Books in the Abundant Freedom Series

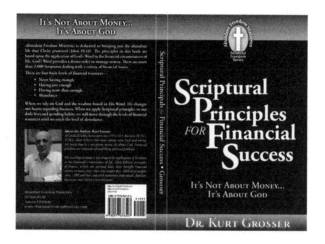

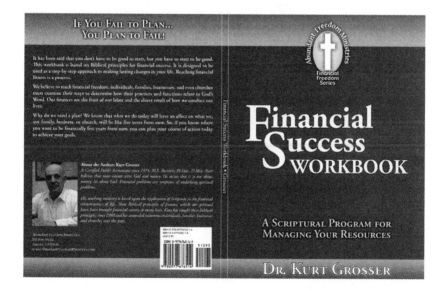

For further information about our Ministry and Publications visit
our Web site, www.AbundantFreedomMinistries.com
or write to Abundant Freedom Press,
P.O. Box 461316, Aurora, Colorado 80046